Experience
Royal Dornoch

by *OptimizeGolf*

"This book is dedicated to the enchanting
swathe of land on a remote Scottish shore
that is Royal Dornoch Golf Club.
It is not a historical reference book.
Instead, the intention is to capture the charm
of the Royal Burgh and to portray the unique
character of a course which enhances
the great traditions of Scottish links golf."

Published by:

Personal Navigation Systems Ltd., Roseberry Court, Ellerbeck Way, Stokesley Business Park, Cleveland, TS9 5QT, United Kingdom.

Printed and bound in the Czech Republic.

ISBN: 0-9550041-0-1

Bibliography:

A History of The Royal Dornoch Golf Club 1877-1999 by Dr. John Macleod.

Pictures by:
David Scaletti   - 4.
St Andrews University Library - 8.
Andrew Carnegie Birthplace Museum - 11.
Glyn Satterley   - Sleeve, 6, 7, 9, 10, 16, 18, 19, 28, 29, 30, 31, 34, 35, 37,
                 42, 43, 45, 51, 52, 53, 55, 62, 63, 72, 73, 76, 82, 83, 92, 93.
Eric Hepworth   - 12, 13, 17, 23, 33, 47, 68, 91, 94.
Scottish Viewpoint Picture Library - 14.
Fotografix Scotland - 14, 15.
Craig Mackay   - 37.

Acknowledgements

Thanks are due to many people for their help in producing this unique book, in particular the following people:

Richard Goodale has been a member of Royal Dornoch for 25 years and knows the course intimately. His literary contribution throughout the book has been immense and we are grateful to him.

Acclaimed golf course photographers Glyn Satterley and Eric Hepworth have provided stunning images of the Championship Course and we thank them for their skill and co-operation.

Andrew Skinner the Club Professional used his vast knowledge of the course to contribute to the hole by hole descriptions which constitute the heart of this book.

Thanks also to the Secretary/Manager John Duncan and his staff for their help and support with the research and production of this book.

Contents:

Gary Wolstenholme

Two times Amateur Champion and five times Walker Cup team member
looks back twenty years to his early experiences of Royal Dornoch.

"My experiences of the glorious golf links at Royal Dornoch begin in the summer of 1985 when I was a competitor in the British Amateur Championship. Then, the beguiling subtleties and intricacies of the course presented the qualifiers with as rigorous a test of golfing skill as they were likely to encounter anywhere in the world.

The course played differently from day to day depending on the wind, but with its slick greens and tricky approaches it retained its integrity throughout the Championship. Individual scores were seldom below par despite the presence in the field of defending champion Jose Maria Olazabal who, in fact, shot an 86 in one round in extremely windy conditions.

I too found the course and conditions very challenging especially on Dunrobin, the par four 8th, which could often offer a birdie opportunity but always threatened a bogey.

Twenty years ago Royal Dornoch was unique amongst contemporary seaside courses because of the magical quality of its natural elements. Seaweed smells from incoming tides, North Sea waves lapping sandy beaches, sea bird song and sea borne sounds filling the sparkling air. Brilliant 'artist's' light, magnificent vistas, subtle hues and splendour, splendour everywhere".

Gary Wolstenholme

Sunrise over the 8th fairway can be as early as 2.30am. This hole proved to be a stiff test for Gary Wolstenholme in 1985.

Foreword

When I first visited Royal Dornoch in 1978, it was meant to be a welcome diversion from the 'main' courses of the central belt of Scotland, a cleanser of the golfing palate, a chance to see the beauty of the Highlands. It turned out to be the jewel in the crown.

Like the other Scottish links of that time, Dornoch was a bit 'rough-and-ready.' Tees and greens seemed to flow into each other and the lines between fairway and rough were not always well defined. The turf was tightly cut and springy, and the ball rarely 'sat up' for you. You had to keep your eye keen and your swing steady, and if you did not, the most embarrassing of foozles could and would occur. On the other hand, if you managed to hit down on the ball and catch it clean, the sight of your ball flying straight towards a far away green against the multi-coloured sky was one that could never be forgotten.

Where Dornoch was different from the other great courses in Scotland was in the character of the light, the air and the people.

The very atmosphere was unique with colours and smells all of their own. It was fresh and pure and even intoxicating.

Today Dornoch has changed in some ways, but in the most important ways it is still the same. The course is slightly more 'polished', but its greatness and mysteries still remain. The Club is a bit more sophisticated, but retains its simple and honest character. The people are more cosmopolitan, but there still is a levelling effect. In Dornoch, Burns' dictum that "a man's a man, for aw that" holds true.

And the air and the light and the smells are still there, and the magic...

Richard Goodale

Experiences Over Time

The remoteness of Dornoch has helped create a mystique about this magnificent golfing outpost in the far north of Scotland. It is fifty miles north of Loch Ness and just 8 degrees south of the Arctic Circle and on a June evening it's possible to play golf until almost midnight.

A Glorious Past

Golf has been played for well over 500 years and Dornoch is one of the few venues in the world which can trace its history back that far. A proper club was not established at Dornoch until 1877, but this was not long after the 'modernisation' of the game had occurred in the latter half of the 19th century, starting with Alan Robertson's work at St. Andrews.

The pivotal event in Dornoch's history was the appointment of John Sutherland as Secretary in 1883. A tireless promoter and gifted architect, Sutherland continued in that role until his death, 58 years later.

During his tenure the Club was transformed from a sleepy local society with a primitive course to a thriving national club with one of the finest courses in Great Britain and the world.

His sense of the importance of agronomy can be seen through his employment of the children and women of nearby Embo to hand pick weeds off the early greens. This is credited with laying the foundation for the magnificent putting surfaces which exist today.

John Sutherland was a regular columnist for two London publications and his writing would have contributed to the influx of prominent visitors from the South that Dornoch enjoyed during the period 1918 - 1939.

Among his many other talents John Sutherland was also a fine player. In the famous 'Dornoch Invasion' of the Amateur Championship at Muirfield in 1909 he made it to the 5th round, beating such players as Harry Colt and Harold Hilton in the process.

John Sutherland's influence extends to:

- Hiring Old Tom Morris to build an extension to 18 proper holes in 1886.

- The establishment of a Ladies course of 5500 yards on the lower links in 1923.

- Improving, enlarging and lengthening the Course in conjunction with his green keepers.

- Establishing Dornoch as a Royal club, after it was granted a Royal Charter by King Edward VII in 1906, and promoting Dornoch as a summer outpost for many prominent golfing families from England, of whom Ernest Holderness and Joyce and Roger Wethered were the most important.

John Sutherland's portrait, by David Alison RSA, hangs by the staircase in the clubhouse.

The Club Captain first presented the Caddies
Cup to the best junior player of the year in 1922.
It is a coveted trophy and still played for today.

Three medals from the year the Club was formed.
The one with a ribbon was the very first
to be struck in 1877.

The Carnegie Connection

Around the turn of the last century another important figure came to Dornoch.

Andrew Carnegie, the son of weavers from Dunfermline, was by then a Scots-American and the richest man in the world. Looking for a place to retire, Carnegie bought nearby Skibo Castle for $2 million, not much to him, even then, but a fortune to many. As his purchase coincided with a generous settlement of a business dispute with one of his partners, he referred to Skibo as "A nice present from Mr. Frick."

Not a golfer but wishing to learn, Carnegie hired John Sutherland to build him a 9-hole course at Skibo, a few holes of which have now been restored and form the basis of what is now the Carnegie Links.

He was a Vice-President of the Club, but his most important legacy to Dornoch is the Carnegie Shield, a magnificent trophy which has been contested since 1901. More about that later. It is fitting that there are two pictures of the Cathedral engraved on it, for not only did Dornoch grow around the medieval Cathedral, but it was the clergy who first introduced golf to Dornoch.

Experiences of Dornoch Today

A view of the peaceful and charming high street.

The Castle Hotel (right) and the old jail.

The Burgh

The Royal Burgh of Dornoch would not seem out of place to our ancestors. The major landmarks such as the Cathedral, the Bishop's Palace (now the Castle Hotel) and Burghfield House look today much as they did then.

Most houses in the centre of the town have hardly changed over the years. It is still possible to see where Donald Ross, the locally born course architect, lived on St. Gilbert's Street before he left for America as a young man. The times are changing though. Over the past 10 - 15 years the population of the town has grown modestly, as retirees from outside of Dornoch move in to enjoy the clean air, the quiet life and the magnificent golf.

There is a real and potential conflict between the legitimate desires of incomers and the needs of the locals who comprise the backbone and the historical conscience of the community. As always, Dornoch is constructive in resolving these tensions.

Dornoch's Cathedral was the scene of Madonna's son Rocco's christening in 2000.

Maintenance work is continuous to keep the course in optimum condition for maximum enjoyment throughout the year.

The Course

If the great players who knew Dornoch around the early 1900's - Ross, Taylor, Herd, Vardon and Massey, were to visit today, they would find the experience in many ways similar to when they were last here, but in other ways very different.

The course would look and feel very familiar off the first tee, with the club house, the two grand hotels and the summer cottages off to the left, and pure linksland tumbling down to the right towards the sea. The sense of splendid isolation which has always defined Dornoch would still be there. That being said, Royal Dornoch is a far different course today than it was in 1905.

Although the course is not significantly longer than it was then, certainly not with the club and ball technologies available today, it nevertheless plays as if it were long, even in little or no breeze. It snakes out towards Embo and back rather than going on to the lower links for its last 6 holes as it did then.

The conditioning, due to modern agronomy and increased budgets, is less variable and the greens staff still strive to keep the course fast and firm, as links courses should be. Putting surfaces are just as true but generally much faster. One wonders how the golden age golfers would have coped with greens "stimping" at 11 or 12? Probably they would have adapted well, as all good sportsmen can and will do.

The exposed plateau of the tricky second green.

The third phase of Royal Dornoch's modern history is the period after the Second World War. In 1945, a third of the Championship Course (then holes 13 - 18) and all of the Ladies Course had been lost to military requisition. To remedy this, in 1946 the Club hired George Duncan to lay out 6 new holes from the point of the current 5th green towards Embo and back. With the considerable help of Robbie Grant and Danny McCulloch, the Green Keeper and Professional at the time, this was accomplished with great skill.

There are many visitors today who marvel at the fact that the magnificent stretch of holes from 6 - 11 at Royal Dornoch are not part of the original course and are 'only' 60 years old.

Future Changes?

At present, nothing architecturally significant is planned for the championship course. Even the simplest of changes is scrutinised with great care and caution. A simple and reasonable proposal to add a new pot bunker at the end of the string of them on the 3rd fairway, to catch masters of the new technology, was turned down at the 2004 AGM. A bolder, but still modest, proposal to open the burn running under the 9th fairway, about 10 yards from the green, was similarly shelved in 2001. Doubtless, there will be a few new 'tiger' tees, and maybe some of these will come more into regular play in the future. However, in general, the Royal Dornoch of 2105 will, justifiably, look much like today.

Looking back along the 5th fairway from the green.

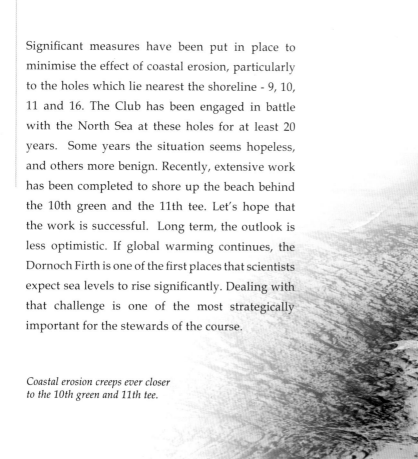

Significant measures have been put in place to minimise the effect of coastal erosion, particularly to the holes which lie nearest the shoreline - 9, 10, 11 and 16. The Club has been engaged in battle with the North Sea at these holes for at least 20 years. Some years the situation seems hopeless, and others more benign. Recently, extensive work has been completed to shore up the beach behind the 10th green and the 11th tee. Let's hope that the work is successful. Long term, the outlook is less optimistic. If global warming continues, the Dornoch Firth is one of the first places that scientists expect sea levels to rise significantly. Dealing with that challenge is one of the most strategically important for the stewards of the course.

Coastal erosion creeps ever closer to the 10th green and 11th tee.

11th Tee

10th Green

The Struie Course

The real change that has occurred and will continue to occur in the future at Dornoch is with the second course, the Struie. This has grown from a 9-hole 'holiday/beginners' course, cobbled together after the war from parts of the Ladies course and the 6 abandoned holes from the 'big' course, to the 6300 yard 'proper' course that it is today. That being said, the Struie still needs finishing if it is to approach the quality of the 'top' course.

As of now it is an amalgam of a few Old Tom Morris holes, some holes built by Donald Steel in the 1980's and 90's and 5 new 'championship' holes designed by Robin Hiseman and put into play in 2003. It meets the needs of the Club for a 'relief' course, but there is still a need for a beginners/holiday 9, much like the old Struie. Fortunately there is ample land for this to be done. When? We shall see.

This hole on the Struie has not been claimed by coastal erosion but, ironically, has become a victim of Health and Safety Regulations due to its close proximity to the road, houses and walkers. It is maintained all year and still used occasionally during the quieter winter months.

Royal Dornoch
Golf Club

Royal Dornoch is a private members club governed by the Captain, Vice Captain and council of nine members. The Secretary/Manager, through the administrative staff, Head Greenkeeper, Greens and House Staff are responsible for the operations of the Club's policy.

The Club has a full membership of 1315 regionally split:

290 resident
155 Highland region
305 rest of Scotland
235 rest of Great Britain
330 overseas

In addition there are 380 non-voting members in the Struie, non-playing and junior categories.

Championship Course

Hole	Yards	SI	Par	Hole	Yards	SI	Par
1 FIRST	331	7	4	10 FUARAN	177	16	3
2 ORD	184	15	3	11 A'CHLACH	450	4	4
3 EARL'S CROSS	414	11	4	12 SUTHERLAND	507	12	5
4 ACHINCHANTER	427	3	4	13 BENTS	180	18	3
5 HILTON	354	9	4	14 FOXY	445	2	4
6 WHINNY BRAE	163	17	3	15 STULAIG	358	10	4
7 PIER	463	1	4	16 HIGH HOLE	402	6	4
8 DUNROBIN	437	5	4	17 VALLEY	405	8	4
9 CRAIGLAITH	529	13	5	18 HOME	456	14	4
OUT 3302			35	IN 3380			35

TOTAL YARDS 6682   PAR 70

A wonderful panoramic view which is so typical of the landscape at Royal Dornoch.

One assumes that the whiskies and beers available in the lounge would taste much the same as they did 100 years ago...

The Clubhouse

The clubhouse itself is still relatively modest, particularly for a golf club of such international prominence. Comfortable rather than grand, it is sized so that it creaks a little at the seams during major events, but retains its sense of intimacy and peace for the large majority of the time when it is less busy.

Over the years the membership of the Club has grown substantially. In 1905 there were just over 100 members, while today there are over 1300. Back then, most members were local, but even by 1913, nearly two thirds were from outside the Highland region. Overseas membership has grown from a handful (even as late as 1977 there were only 13) to 330 or so today.

Dornoch has always had to balance the needs of its visiting and local members. It is a delicate act which, due to its experience in these matters, the Club does well.

In addition to catering for its members the Club entertains in excess of 12,000 visitors per season, which given its location is testament to its international reputation in golf.

The '19th' has a wonderful view of the course.

The Seasons at Dornoch

From October to April, the locals rule the roost. Contrary to some popular belief golf can be played at Dornoch throughout the year, and the middle of winter is often the most satisfying time to play. The course and the town are quiet, the light can be magical and the marvellous greens are in play for all but the most frigid of days. If you are ever there at this time of year make sure you enter the Pro's walk-on Stableford competition on Thursday after lunch. You will learn more about the local members whilst playing golf, and during the banter in the clubhouse afterwards, than can be told in days or even years of writing.

Starting at the Burghfield Open tournament on the May Day weekend, visiting members begin to filter into the town from all over the world. This is Royal Dornoch's first 'major.' Founded by the Currie brothers who owned the Burghfield House Hotel for 50+ years, it is more a gathering of the clans than a competition. The après-golf is at least as important as the golf itself.

In June, the town and the course begins to heave with people with foreign accents and strange golf swings. For the locals and dedicated visitors there is the respite of the Club Championship. The Club reclaims the course from its guests, at least for a short period of time when four rounds of stroke play take place during the week, culminating with 36 holes for the top 12 qualifiers on the Saturday.

The heraldic coat of arms was awarded to the Club by Lord Lyon of Scotland. The Club is careful to allow this only to be used on garments sold to members.

The non-members or visitors logo originates from the time before the Club was awarded 'Royal' status. The dates on the badge reflect the time golf was played over the Dornoch links prior to the formal formation of the Club.

Take time out to appreciate the magnificent panoramic views like this one looking across the 14th green.

The greenkeeping staff maintain the course in prime condition for the summer tournaments.

The height of the summer golf season is mid-July, when the third major, the Sinclair Cup takes place. An open tournament with 36 holes of strokeplay for scratch to 20+ handicappers.

Last but not least, the most important one of all, is Andrew Carnegie's 'Shield.' For a week in early August, 360 are chosen to play, roughly two thirds of which are low handicap players (+3 to 9) and the rest double digits. There are two qualifying rounds of strokeplay, from which the top 32 players compete off scratch in matchplay, for the Shield itself.

With so many players around for such a long time, the Shield is a memorable spectacle. On the first 4 days of qualifying there is an eerie mixture of friendship and terror. It is great to see so many old friends again, but last thing you want to do is walk into the clubhouse and have to answer the

question "So, how did you do?!" when you just signed for an 85... or 95 or even 75, depending on your ability and ambitions.

Once the cut is made for the Shield, Thursday is sorting out day. The lesser players are eliminated and assume traditional roles of court jester, petulant loser and/or 'eminence grise'. Friday, when there are two matches to play, is when the tournament proper really starts. This is a very peaceful time at Dornoch. There are fewer and fewer matches on the course and so many unsuccessful players have left for their homes that only the locals and the hard core remain to watch the drama unfold.

It is extremely bright in mid-August in Dornoch, and you can sit in the clubhouse until 10pm and see the amazing contours of the links grow out of the lengthening shadows.

Andrew Carnegie presented this shield to the club
for annual competition in 1901.

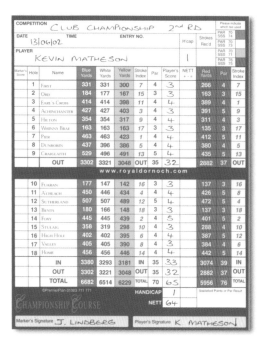

Kevin Matheson set the amateur course record of 65 in the second round of the Club Championship in 2002. His round is shown on the next page.

The professional course record of 62 was set by Stephen Gray-Hayston in the second round of the Royal Dornoch Assistants Masters in 1999.

COMPETITION ROYAL DORNOCH ASSISTANTS MASTERS - ROUND 2
DATE 28/9/99 **TIME** 10:03 **ENTRY NO.**
PLAYER STEPHEN GRAY - HAYSTON

Marker's Score	Hole	Name	Blue Yards	White Yards	Yellow Yards	Stroke Index	Par	Player's Score	NETT POINTS	Ladie's Yards	Par	L.O.U. Index
	1	First	331	331	300	7	4	5		266	4	7
	2	Ord	184	177	167	15	3	3		163	3	15
	3	Earl's Cross	414	414	398	11	4	5		389	4	1
	4	Achinchanter	427	427	403	3	4	5		391	5	9
	5	Hilton	354	354	317	9	4	5		311	4	3
	6	Whinny Brae	163	163	163	17	3	5		135	3	17
	7	Pier	463	463	423	1	4	5		412	5	11
	8	Dunrobin	437	396	386	5	4	4		380	4	5
	9	Craiglaith	529	496	447	13	5	4		435	5	13
	OUT		3302	3321	3004	OUT	35	29		2882	37	OUT
	10	Fuaran	177	147	142	16	3	5		137	3	16
	11	A'chlach	450	446	434	4	4	5		426	5	4
	12	Sutherland	557	507	489	12	5	5		472	5	12
	13	Bents	180	166	148	18	3	2		137	3	18
	14	Foxy	445	445	439	2	4	5		401	5	2
	15	Stulaig	358	319	298	10	4	4		288	4	10
	16	High Hole	402	402	395	6	4	4		387	5	6
	17	Valley	405	405	390	8	4	5		384	4	8
	18	Home	456	456	446	14	4	4		442	5	14
	IN		3380	3293	3181	IN	35	33		3074	39	IN
	OUT		3302	3321	3004	OUT	35	29		2882	37	OUT
	TOT		6732	6514	6185	TOT	70	62		5956	76	TOT

PLEASE AVOID SLOW PLAY AT ALL TIMES

HANDICAP
NETT

Player's Signature .... Marker's Signature ....

Saturday morning of the Shield brings even fewer people to the course. The twelve semi-finalists from the three categories of competition go off on their own, followed only by family, friends and stray dogs. At 2pm or so, however, people desert the town for the first tee. Coming out to watch the Shield final is a highlight of the Highland social calendar. There are usually 100-200 people following the final match, most of whom are serious golfers, but more than a few of whom are just locals who want to be a part of the spectacle. It is rare, however, that the golf played in the final is anything more than very competent. Perhaps it is the pressure of the event, but level par will usually prevail.

Nevertheless, the list of winners of the event is awesome. International players such as Wethered and Holderness. Players such as Jimmy Miller (Brora) who was probably as good as any true amateur golfer in the world in the years between 1965 and 1985. 'Locals' such as Bill Walker and Willie Skinner and Tommy McCulloch and 'Barrell' and 'Tight' and far too many others to mention. There have also been as many great players who have not won the Shield and these are too numerous to mention.

After the Shield, visitors take to the course again and Dornoch remains busy until after October when it drifts towards the quiet somnolence of winter. The Pro's winter stableford starts and continues through to the Thursday before the Burghfield Open in the spring, when the cycle starts all over again...

The serenity of the course can be enjoyed during an evening stroll any time of the year.

Kevin Matheson's course record of 65 is graphically shown here on a layout of the course.

1 Green in regulation, one putt for a birdie start.

2 Tee shot holds the green, two putts for par.

3 Green in regulation, two putts for par.

4 Green in regulation, one putt for birdie.

5 Green in regulation, two putts for par.

6 Tee shot finds bunker, good recovery shot for par.

7 Green in regulation, two putts for par.

8 Green in regulation, two putts for par.

9 On the green for two, two putts for birdie.

Kevin Matheson
Club Championship - 2nd Round - 13th June 2002

Hole	Yards	SI	Par	Gross Score		Hole	Yards	SI	Par	Gross Score
1 FIRST	331	7	4	3		10 FUARAN	177	16	3	3
2 ORD	184	15	3	3		11 A'CHLACH	450	4	4	4
3 EARL'S CROSS	414	11	4	4		12 SUTHERLAND	507	12	5	4
4 ACHINCHANTER	427	3	4	3		13 BENTS	180	18	3	3
5 HILTON	354	9	4	4		14 FOXY	445	2	4	5
6 WHINNY BRAE	163	17	3	3		15 STULAIG	358	10	4	3
7 PIER	463	1	4	4		16 HIGH HOLE	402	6	4	4
8 DUNROBIN	437	5	4	4		17 VALLEY	405	8	4	3
9 CRAIGLAITH	529	13	5	4		18 HOME	456	14	4	4
OUT 3302		35		32		IN 3380		35		33

TOTAL YARDS 6682   PAR 70   GROSS SCORE 65   NETT SCORE 64

10 Green in regulation, two putts for par.

11 Green in regulation, two putts for par.

12 Reaches the fringe in two, two putts for birdie.

13 Green in regulation, two putts for par.

14 Green in regulation, three putts for bogey.

15 Green in regulation, one putt for birdie.

16 Green in regulation, two putts for par.

17 Green in regulation, one putt for birdie.

18 Green in regulation, two putts for par.

A Hole-By-Hole Tour

This section of the book is not meant to be a definitive guide to the course but rather a light-hearted tour.

It contains descriptions of each hole and helpful advice on how best to play them.

There are also some amusing stories about members and visitors which have taken place over the past 25 years. Andrew Skinner, the Professional at the Club, often recalls the time he teed off with a consenting member called Don Greenberg at 2.40 in the morning and played 7 rounds in one day finishing at 9.45 in the evening!

All distances are measured in yards.

41

Holes 1, 2 & 3

First, Ord, Earl's Cross

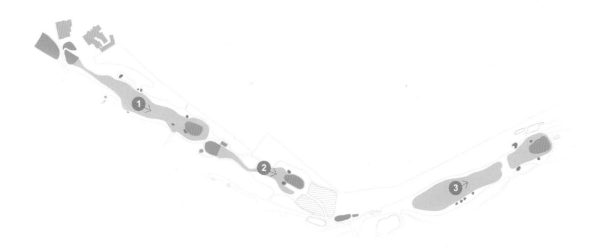

The Dornoch experience begins...

Standing on the 1st tee one might wonder just why the long journey to the heart of the Highlands was made. The clubhouse is modest, the views over the sea are only serene and the hole in front of you seems to be just a drive and a pitch. But as you mark a 5 on your card you convince yourself that this was just an anomaly. Then you confront the 2nd, sheltered from the sea, quite possibly hit your ball on the green and 2-putt for a par. It all seems so homely and simple and then you walk through the whins to see the magnificence of the links.

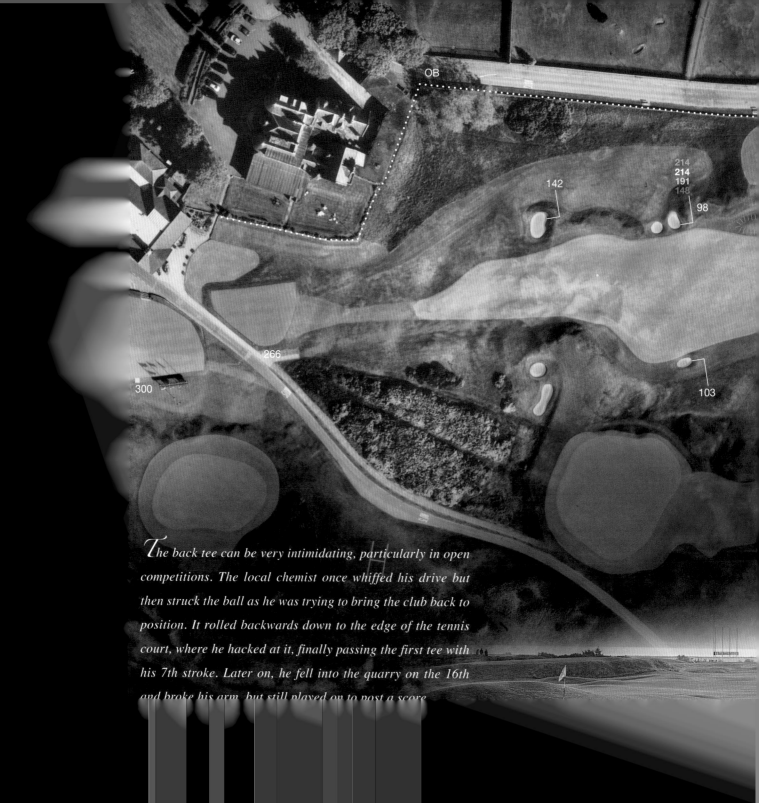

OB

214
214
191
148

142

98

103

266

300

The back tee can be very intimidating, particularly in open competitions. The local chemist once whiffed his drive but then struck the ball as he was trying to bring the club back to position. It rolled backwards down to the edge of the tennis court, where he hacked at it, finally passing the first tee with his 7th stroke. Later on, he fell into the quarry on the 16th and broke his arm, but still played on to post a score.

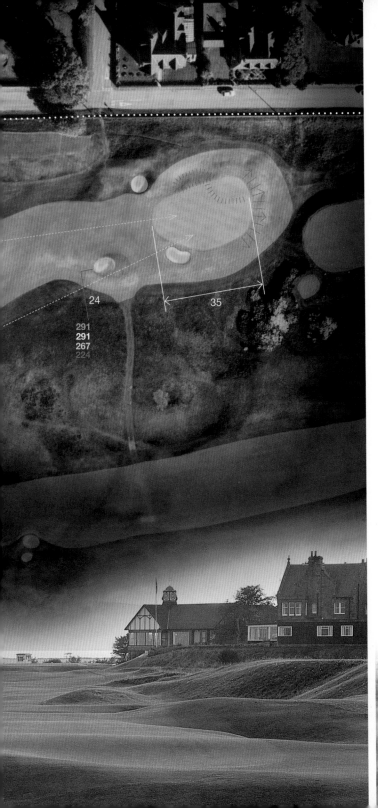

1 *First*

■□ 331 ■ 300 ■ 266 • Par 4

The first is a gentle opener, perhaps the best birdie opportunity on the course, and yet 5 strokes or more are far too possible. It should be no more than a drive and a wedge, with a premium for going down the left side as this opens up the green.

From the medal tees, the fairway bunkers on the left come into play especially into a wind. Miss the fairway left and a blind shot to the green out of thick rough is likely. Miss it right and a difficult pitch over two bunkers looms. Even from the middle of the fairway the pitch is difficult as the green is hard and fast and falls off sharply at the back and sides. There are two great pin positions, one long right and the other middle left which will test even the best, as a straight putt is rare, even from two or three feet from the hole.

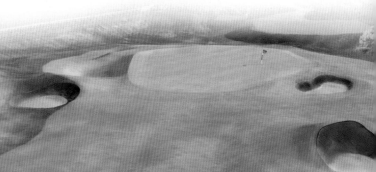

Count yourself lucky that these days there is a fringe around the green. In the early 80's the banks were shaved as close as Kojak's head, and going back and forth across the green was very possible. A 'local' walking his dog once encountered an Irish friend walking to the third in the morning round of a 36-hole competition, and asked how he was doing. "I've just taken a 17 and I've 34 more holes to play!"

177   167   163

184

OB

165
156
148

40

■ 184 □ 177 ■ 167 ■ 163 • Par 3

This is a fantastic par 3 and depending on the wind may require anything from a pitching wedge to a driver. It should be a relatively straight forward mid iron shot to the green if it was not for the fact that the green is an exposed plateau, eighteen yards wide and guarded by two of the largest bunkers on the course. The left and rear of the green slope down six feet or more to an area of thick grass whereas the right slopes down to closely mown fairway. From either side you are left scratching your head, wondering how you are going to play the shot, a bump and run into the bank or a 'Michelson' flop shot. The green itself slopes sharply from left to right towards the sea and from back to front. Hit the green and you're laughing. Miss the green and you are left with one of the hardest shots in golf. When people ask, "What is the most difficult shot at Dornoch?" the reply is often "The second to the 2nd".

414 398 389

133

262
262
247
237

170

227
227
212
203

There is a bunker on the 3rd which sits in the left rough about 15 yards short of the green and can be reached only by the execution of 2 (or more) truly dreadful shots. Nevertheless, in those extremely rare occasions that it is reached, the challenge facing you is superb - a long bunker shot over rough which must be played left of the bunker guarding the left hand side of the green. Superfluous bunkers like this are very much a part of what makes golf so fascinating.

$\mathcal{3}$ Earl's Cross

■□ 414 ■ 398 ■ 389 • Par 4

As you leave the second green you walk through whins. Suddenly the true splendour of the course bursts out in front of you. From the tee you can see more than half of the course and if you are lucky enough to be there in the spring, when the whins are in bloom, the scene is like no other.

Sloping banks of gorse line the entire length of the left side of the hole thus, psychologically, setting up a tee shot that favours the right. However, the fairway slopes from left to right and a good tee shot should be hit over the large mound on the left side of the fairway. Anything hit to the right side of the fairway will be naturally drawn to the four bunkers.

Earl's Cross

The second shot depends on the execution of the drive. If you are playing your second from the rough on the left, you should aim short of the left greenside bunker. You will see your ball move sharply right towards the centre of the green. If you've driven to position 'A', alongside the last fairway bunker on the right, you can fire a mid iron straight for the middle of the green.

Four bunkers lie in wait for any shot straying to the right.

Holes 4, 5 & 6
Achinchanter, Hilton, Whinny Brae

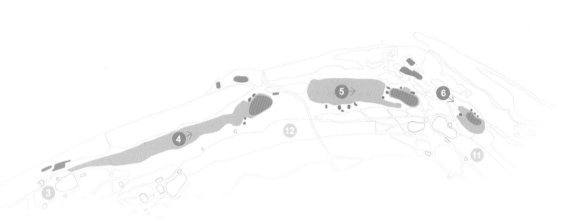

An unforgettable trio...

You are in the middle of the course and an integral part of it. From the 4th tee you can see the approach shots to the 3rd green, the players coming up to the 12th green and those teeing off at the 14th. On the 5th you can see well over half of the course, and share your driving space with the 12th. On the 6th you can see shots to the 5th and 11th greens. Each of these holes is a gem in its own right, but the sense of communality is what distinguishes this group.

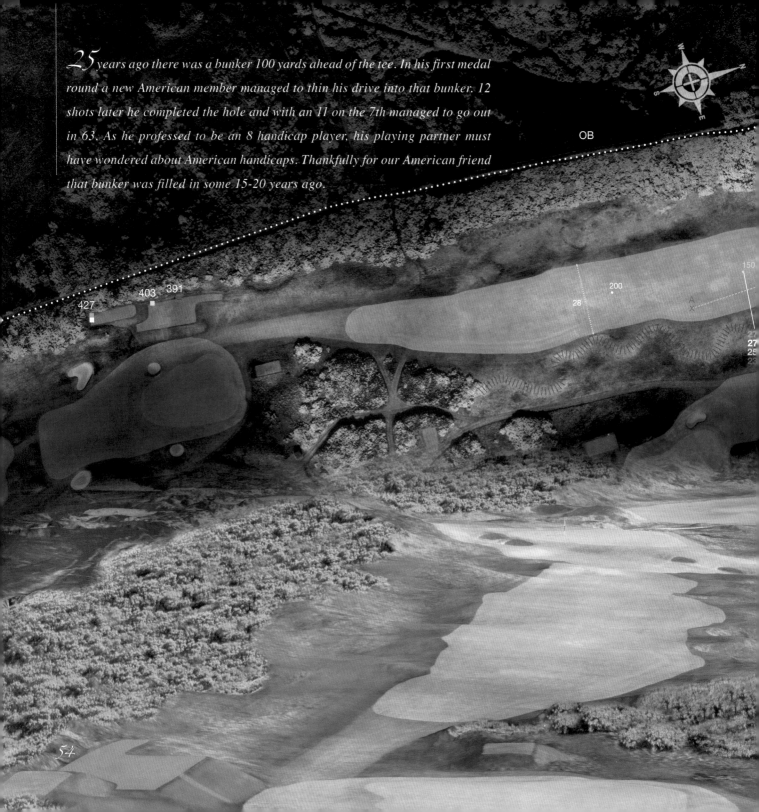

25 years ago there was a bunker 100 yards ahead of the tee. In his first medal round a new American member managed to thin his drive into that bunker. 12 shots later he completed the hole and with an 11 on the 7th managed to go out in 63. As he professed to be an 8 handicap player, his playing partner must have wondered about American handicaps. Thankfully for our American friend that bunker was filled in some 15-20 years ago.

OB

427

403

391

200

28

150

A
X

27
25
23

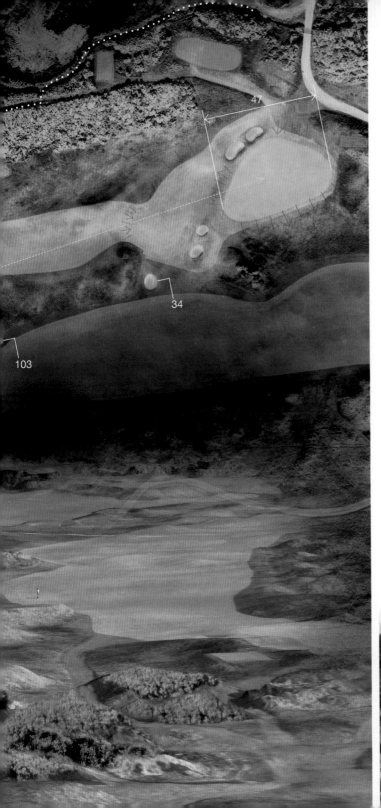

4 *Achinchanter*

■□ 427 ■ 403 ■ 391 • Par 4

As with the 3rd, the 4th is lined with thick gorse along the left side and naturally opens out to the right.

This is a good driving hole and full of great features; a sharply canted fairway framed by natural grassy hollows on each side; a steep dip across the fairway starting 40 or 50 yards short of and extending all the way to a large and undulating green.

Holding a drive on the fairway requires a controlled shot down the left hand side, as the fairway slopes from left to right. Missing the fairway either side will leave a very difficult second from down a steep slope or the grassy hollows.

The best approach to the green is from the right and some locals even aim for the 12th fairway from the tee to avoid all the trouble. From the left, a low punchy running shot through the dip and between the bunkers may be the only way of staying on the green which is so large that three putting is a real possibility.

OB

354

317   311

150

115

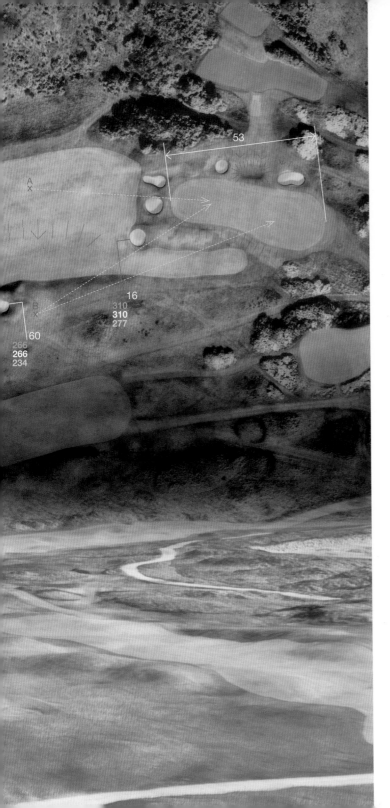

Hilton

■□ 354 ■ 317 ■ 311 • Par 4

This hole is one of those short par 4's that would be a delight on any course. From a highly elevated tee a wide fairway is framed by a hill of rough and whins on the left and a long string of bunkers on the right. The long, elevated and kidney-shaped green is clearly seen and is set at a sharp angle from left to right.

Your ideal tee shot is down the left side of the fairway from which the ball will kick straight, towards the green. The whins on the left seem perilously close and a slightly pulled drive would be severely punished. There is an ocean of space down the right but beware, the fairway slopes quite severely from left to right, along it's central spine. The five perfectly placed bunkers seem to gather any drive hit right of centre.

The elevated green is guarded by bunkers on the front and left and a steep, five or six foot drop-off on the right.

Hilton

The approach to the green is usually no more than a wedge, although the difficulty of the shot can vary tremendously depending on which side of the green the approach is made. From the ideal position, left/centre of the fairway, it is a relatively simple pitch down the full length of the green. If you are approaching from the right the shot is much more difficult. You have to hit the ball hard enough to carry the slope along the right but not so hard as to run off into one of the two bunkers or the grassy hollow on the left.

*T*here is one almost unplayable pin position on the hole and that is mid-right, hard against the indentation in the 'kidney.' Any approach shot landing to the right of this will roll off onto the lower fairway 'finger'. One visiting golfer once played safely short and centre of that pin position in two after his opponent missed the green and was facing an impossible shot. His caddie told him "You can't go too far left on this putt!" He pushed it right, it trickled off the green, he halved the hole and eventually lost the match.

163

135

163

12

33

150
150
146
120

One day, Yours Truly was playing in a threesome with an Important Member and a Distinguished Visitor whose bag was carried by a Charismatic Caddy. YT and IM managed to hit the green, but DV fluffed his tee shot into a very difficult lie from which he managed to hit a remarkable recovery shot to 10 feet. IM said to DV, "Greg Norman couldn't have done that any better!" Whereupon CC muttered, "Och, Aye, but Greg Norman never would have been there in the first place!"

6 *Whinny Brae*

■□ 163 ■ 163 ■ 135 • Par 3

Arguably one of the best short holes on the planet, built to make up for the holes lost when the lower linksland at Dornoch was used in WWII for a reserve airfield. Visually, the hole is stunning. From an elevated tee the view of the green is framed by whins both to the left and the rear and the sweep of the magnificent 11th to the right. Three bunkers guard the left side and a large bunker and steep slope guards the right.

The strategy is simple "HIT THE GREEN, STUPID!" Failing to execute this strategy can leave you with all sorts of challenges like hacking out of the whins or hitting a softly, softly shot from one of the pot bunkers on the left. Or, most likely, trying to hit a flop shot up a steep slope off a bare lie to the right that will test even the very best wedge or sand wedge players. As you play the hole you feel you are a part of golf and a part of nature, and if you have been so lucky as to have hit the green, you are particularly blessed.

Holes 7, 8 & 9

Pier, Dunrobin, Craiglaith

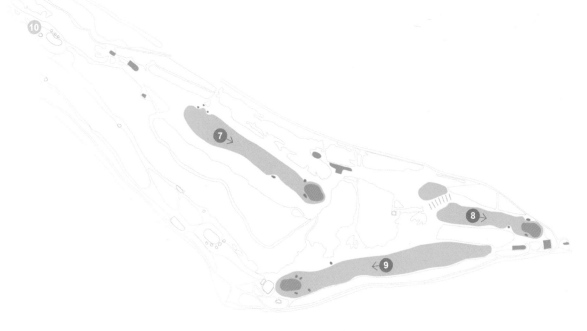

The experience continues...

From the 6th you walk up a steep and narrow path, seemingly away from the golf course and into the bowels of the whins. Then, at the top, you find yourself on the upper plateau, confronted with a heathland vista which then suddenly plummets back to the lower links in the middle of the 8th hole. From there you head back to the clubhouse along the North Sea. It is not until later that you realise that the 9th is the first (and in many ways the only) seaside hole at Dornoch, so pervasive are the views and sense of presence of the sea. As you count your score for the front 9, you realise that any number starting with a '3' is a fine achievement.

The legendary local hotelier, Euan Currie joined Richard Goodale and two other friends one day for a game. As they were walking up the hill after the 6th, a loud shout was heard. Somebody had made a hole-in-one. On the 7th tee Euan reached into his bag and produced a linen table cloth, 4 crystal glasses and a bottle of Macallan. When the group behind arrived, Euan simply said "Congratulations", offered the bewildered Canadians a dram, and they are probably still wondering what hit them to this day....

OB

311
270

226

200

423 412

463

7 *Pier*

■□ 463 ■ 423 ■ 412 • Par 4

There is a long steep climb up the hill from the 6th to the 7th tee. Once there you are both breathless and back on the raised beach of the first and second holes. This is rated stroke index 1 at Royal Dornoch although most visitors find 'Foxy', hole 14, the most difficult. Whins line both sides of the fairway and over the past twenty years have been cut back substantially to make the hole more playable. Consequently this has made the hole less intimidating from the championship tee.

Nevertheless, three fairway bunkers to the left at approximately 220 yards are to be avoided if you are to reach the green in two. More often than not a long second shot is required and if under hit will not make it up the steep slope at the front of the green. Two bunkers, left and right, protect a slightly raised and undulating green. If you miss the green in two then a top class short game is needed to get up and down.

"*Many locals do not like the medal tee, partly because it is "new" (mid-80's) and probably because it is significantly more difficult than the old one. They'll say "It's not 'the 8th'" as if the hole had an existence outside of what man chose and chooses to do with the land. When Tom Watson played Dornoch in 1981, going out into a stiff breeze, he couldn't make it over the plateau, but then hit a magnificent 3-wood onto the green. Now that's golf!*" Richard Goodale

265
225
215
209 152 path

200

168
post

246
206
195
190

150

396 386 380

437

WH

66

OB

38

20

8 *Dunrobin*

■ 437 □ 396 ■ 386 ■ 380 • Par 4

From the tee the 8th consists of a skyline fairway, framed by whins on the right and the old railway line on the left. Ahead is a cliff, a marker post, the old fishing pier at Embo, Dunrobin Castle and the North Sea. The fairway extends along the upland plateau before plunging over a 40 foot cliff to the linksland below. Once over the hill, you will find yourself on the loveliest and lumpiest of fairways you can imagine, facing a semi-blind shot to a punchbowl green.

From the medal tee, the best line is over the marker post, but the drive must be long and straight. From the front tees the drive requires a straight shot of just 200 yards or so to reach the slope and down to the lower fairway. As with all such shots, there is a thrill in approaching the ridge to see where your second shot has finished.

Dunrobin

When you have hit a perfect drive over the marker post and from the ridge above you see your ball on the fairway, you may think, "Great, I've only a wedge to the green". When you get to your ball you then think "How on earth I am I going to play this?" More than likely you will not be able to see the surface of the green and you will certainly be hitting off a very severe slope. Fortunately, the green gathers shots so the approach can be played short and left to chase onto the bowl like putting surface. This is one of the fastest greens on the course and hitting that six foot birdie putt six feet past the hole is very possible.

The approach to the green from one of the most undulating fairways you'll encounter.

LH

200

330
298
290
286

263 path

435

254
219
214
160

496 491

529

This is the first hole where the omnipresent sea is directly encountered. Playing back to the fairway from the sands off the 9th is one of the more thrilling shots in golf. Scuba divers off the shore report stories of huge pools of golf balls rolling back and forth with the tides in large rock pools at the bottom of the sea.

9 Craiglaith

■529 □496 ■491 ■435 • Par 5

You are now turning 'home' and for the first time directly by the sea which runs beside you all the way to the green. The fairway is steeply undulating but there is a fifteen yard wide 'fast lane' on the far left wedged between the right hand lumps and the marram grass bordering the sea. If you can hit that channel with power, your ball will bound forward into mid-iron range.

If, however, you drive 'safely' to the right, getting on in two is problematic. You will have a long shot from an uneven lie and the two deep bunkers to the right of the green come very much into play. Once there, the green is relatively flat but long. Like the 1st, this may be a good birdie opportunity but far too often you will have a tricky five footer for par.

Holes 10, 11 & 12

Fuaran, A'chlach, Sutherland

On your way in....

The 10th, 11th and 12th continue the path back home along the lower links, moving subtly but increasingly inland so that the most immature dunes begin to separate and protect the course from the sea. To the left of the 10th green and 11th tee, the power of the sea can be seen, as well as the attempts of man to mitigate this power. As the 12th wends its way away from the North Sea, you can understand some of the genius of Old Tom Morris' original design. Holes built closer to the sea might have been more spectacular, but one wonders how long they could have survived if required to share their space with the North Sea.

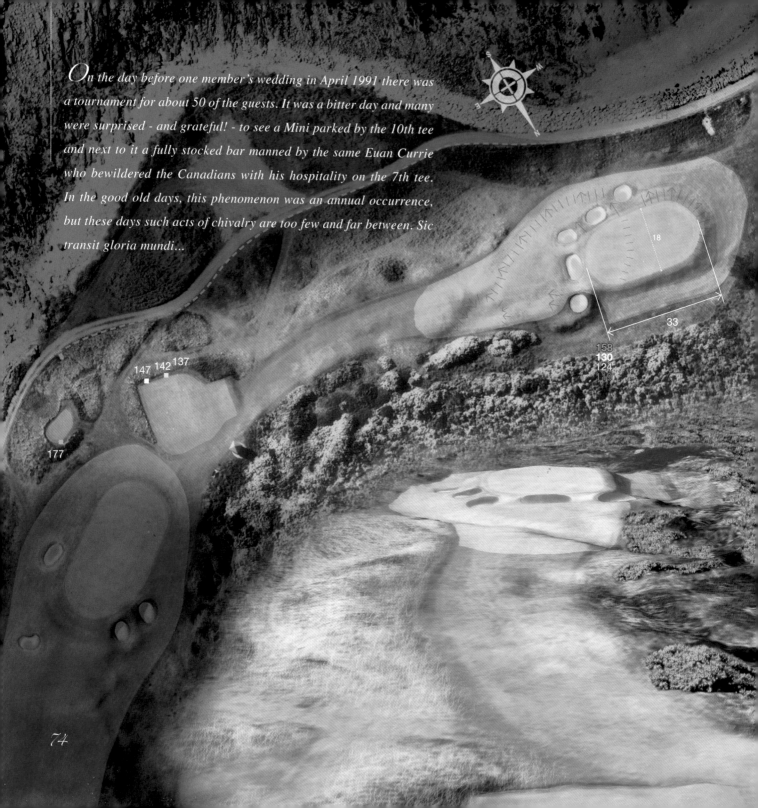

On the day before one member's wedding in April 1991 there was a tournament for about 50 of the guests. It was a bitter day and many were surprised - and grateful! - to see a Mini parked by the 10th tee and next to it a fully stocked bar manned by the same Euan Currie who bewildered the Canadians with his hospitality on the 7th tee. In the good old days, this phenomenon was an annual occurrence, but these days such acts of chivalry are too few and far between. Sic transit gloria mundi...

18

33

158
130
124

147 142 137

177

74

10 *Fuaran*

■ 177 □ 147 ■ 142 ■ 137 • Par 3

Looks simple but plays hard. From the tee it is slightly downhill to a two-tier green raised off of a dip in the land. The hole seems surrounded by bunkers, but the little grassy hollow to the right is a far more troublesome place to be. There is a distinct, though hardly visible right to left cant to the green. If the pin is on the lower tier and you can hit a short iron straight, you will have a very makeable birdie putt. If the pin is on the upper tier, getting the distance right is a challenge.

The wind can make a big difference on this hole. Often a 9-iron is sufficient but it can be as much as a 4-iron into a strong breeze. When downwind and firm, keeping the ball on the green can be nearly impossible. And hitting into the front bunkers may be the best option. On the green, any putt between tiers requires a delicate touch, and all putts on the upper tier are difficult due to the slopes.

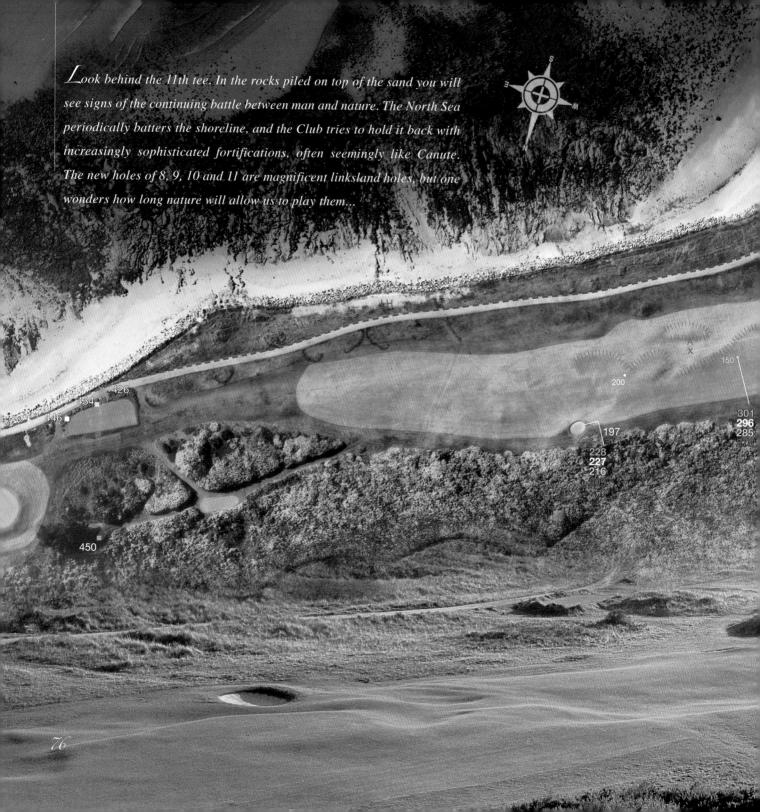

Look behind the 11th tee. In the rocks piled on top of the sand you will see signs of the continuing battle between man and nature. The North Sea periodically batters the shoreline, and the Club tries to hold it back with increasingly sophisticated fortifications, often seemingly like Canute. The new holes of 8, 9, 10 and 11 are magnificent linksland holes, but one wonders how long nature will allow us to play them...

446

434   426

450

200

150

197

228
227
216

301
296
285

11 A'chlach

■ 450 □ 446 ■ 434 ■ 426 • Par 4

One of the toughest holes on the course. The fairway slopes from right to left and getting a flat lie for your second is best assured by going right. This, however is the 'slow lane' and increases the difficulty of the angle of the second shot, particularly if the pin is on the right. Hitting your drive down the middle is likely to gain extra distance from being propelled by the undulating fairway. Your ball is also likely to end up on the left side which is a better angle to the green but here you will be lucky to have a level lie.

The green is deceptively long with all the trouble at the front and plenty of space at the back so it is always wise to take one more club than you think.

Looking back down the 11th fairway towards the tee with the 6th green in the background.

A'chlach

The green is protected by a tongue of land at the approach area which casts off all shots landing short and slightly off line. Because of this feature, ALWAYS take at least one more club and try to carry the front of the green - there is lots of room at the back. There are a number of very good pin positions on the green, particularly mid-left and mid-right just passed the bunker.

The 12th green melds into the 14th medal tee, and that spot is a prime area for watching golf at Dornoch, particularly during open tournaments when you are likely to see some good players. From that area you can see the approaches into 12th, the shots to the green at 13th, the tee shots from 14th and the second shots into 4th. On a clear day there are few places better to be on this earth.

507

507   489   472

200

254 path

300
290
280

12 *Sutherland*

■ 507 □ 507 ■ 489 ■ 472 • Par 5

This is one of the few holes on the course where you can 'open up your shoulders' as there is miles of room right in case you come off the ball. The cardinal sin is to go left, as you will find yourself in the dunes with a problem in getting it out far enough to reach the green in three. To achieve position 'A' aim at the mound of whins on the right side of the fairway. A good drive will leave you 200 - 220 yards to a green guarded on the right by a gathering bunker and on the left by a 10-foot high dune which considerably narrows the entrance to the green.

The elegant option is a high fade over the hump. The canny one is a run up with a bit of draw. If you cannot reach the green in two, the third shot offers the full range of short-game possibilities, from putting to chipping or pitching. This is a birdie opportunity if you hit a good drive, but one where a six is very, very possible if you find the rough.

Holes 13, 14 & 15

Bents, Foxy, Stulaig

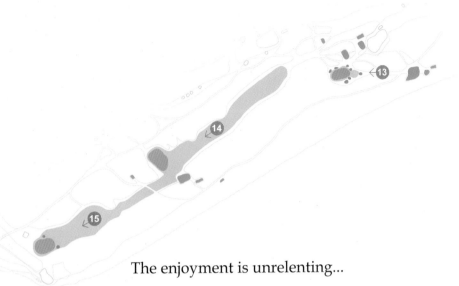

The enjoyment is unrelenting...

The 13th brings you briefly back to the dune ridge. If you climb it from the tee to check the wind (as you should) you are standing at the edge of Dornoch's spectacular beach. On the rare days when it is calm and warm, no shore in the Caribbean could be as pleasant. As you view the emptiness of the strand you give thanks to the fact that it is not always so calm and warm. A beach so beautiful would not be the same if full of people. The tee shot is back into the middle of the course, and then the 14th and 15th straddle the transition between the lower and middle plateaux of the links. Each of the greens of these two holes are sited on that magical middle ridge. Foxy, the 14th is legendary but the 15th, in its own way, is equally as good.

*O*ne of the better local golfers once went 1, 3 on 13 and 14. When he got back to the clubhouse, someone said to him "I can understand the hole-in-one on the 13th, but how in hell did you get a 3 on Foxy!

36

162
148
129

137

166

148

180

13 Bents

■ 180 □ 166 ■ 148 ■ 137 • Par 3

The last of the short holes, and the easiest by far. An elevated tee in the dunes to a well bunkered punchbowl green. (Helpful hint: the hole is sheltered from the wind so go up to the dune overlooking the beach to see how it is REALLY blowing). If you hit the tee shot reasonably straight, with the right club, your ball will not end up far from the pin. If you do miss the green, getting up and down from the left is difficult, but almost impossible from the deep hollow on the right.

The green has subtle contours that make even short putts difficult, particularly if the pin has been cut near the slopes at the sides of the green, as it normally will be. Nevertheless, you should get a 3 and maybe even a 2.

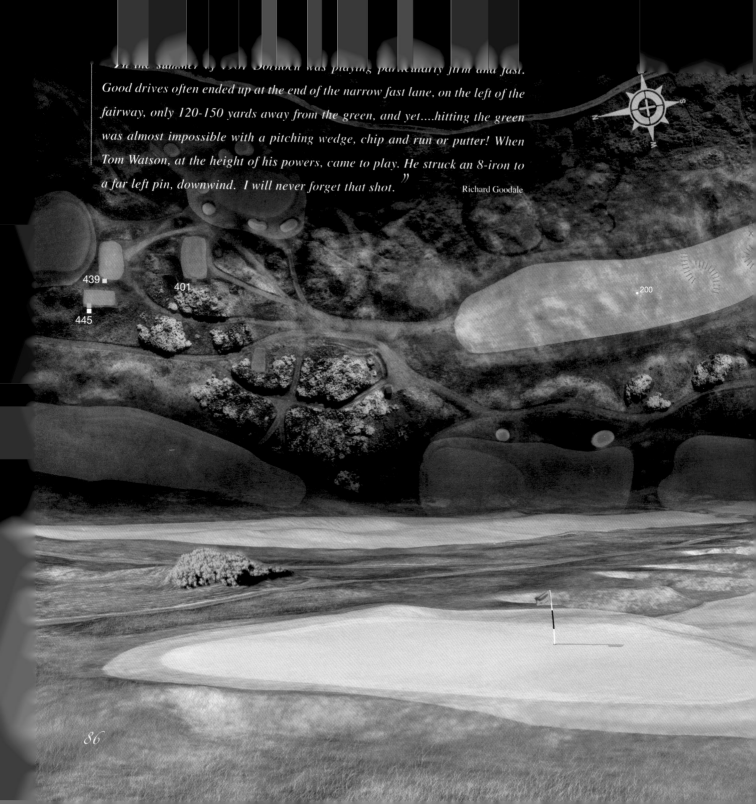

In the summer of 1969 Dornoch was playing particularly firm and fast. Good drives often ended up at the end of the narrow fast lane, on the left of the fairway, only 120-150 yards away from the green, and yet....hitting the green was almost impossible with a pitching wedge, chip and run or putter! When Tom Watson, at the height of his powers, came to play. He struck an 8-iron to a far left pin, downwind. I will never forget that shot. "

Richard Goodale

439

401

445

200

86

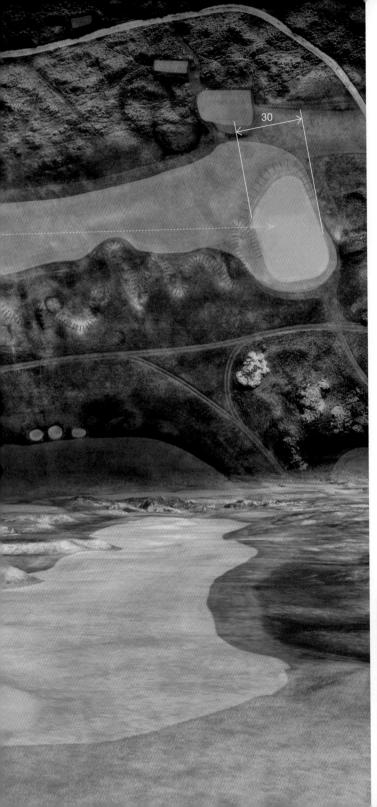

14 *Foxy*

■□445 ■439 ■401 • Par 4

'Foxy' is the most famous hole on the course. A bunker free double-dog leg, (right, left, right) hole sculptured by the ridge of dunes along the right. The main feature visible from the tee is the first of the dunes which juts out into the fairway at approximately 290 yards. A good drive aimed at this dune will leave you in the middle of the fairway but facing a blind second to the green. There is a narrow 'fast lane' down the left side of the fairway which, if hit, can propel your ball to a spot parallel to the dune and giving you a clear 150 yard shot to the green. Anything hit right from the tee will force you to lay up and face a very delicate pitch to the elevated green. The fun begins when you play your second or third or fourth to the green. The green is raised about 5-7 feet above the fairway and all the approaches and run offs are shaved to near green speed.

Elevated view from the men's yellow tee overlooking the ladies tee.

Foxy

There is a large hump at the front centre of the green which throws off slightly inaccurate run-up shots with disdain. Run-up shots hit to the left will roll off towards the 15th tee if not hit perfectly. The right side of the green is protected by the last of the row of dunes. You can, of course, try to fly the ball onto the green, but the green is narrow from front to back and during summer conditions it would be difficult to hold the putting surface. The green is highly contoured and very wide so if you find yourself on the wrong side 3 putting is a distinct possibility.

One member remembers playing in the Shield against a long ago former champion and was looking to win the 15th to square the match. The former champion was lying in three 60 yards out, while the member was 20 yards ahead of him in one. The former champion took out his putter and stroked the ball across all the humps and hollows, up the front slope, around the edge of the right-hand bunker to 6-inches from the pin. The member took four more shots and eventually lost the match...

358

319

298 288

150

90

15 _Stulaig_

■ 358 □ 319 ■ 298 ■ 288 • Par 4

272
234
214
204

64

38

The 15th is a very underrated hole. The main feature off the tee is the 10 - 15 foot dune in the middle of the fairway at about 220 yards. In normal conditions, the good player will carry it, but it can be a severe impediment to the higher handicapper or to anybody if facing a strong wind.

The ideal tee shot is over the right side of the sand dune as there is more room than you think. The approach is the tricky part as the green is raised and like an upturned saucer which will repel even a slightly inaccurate approach. The green is guarded by two bunkers and a steep slope at the front so a run up shot is often the right option. Although the predominant slope is right to left, other, more subtle slopes around the edges make putting a real challenge.

Holes 16, 17 & 18
High Hole, Valley, Home

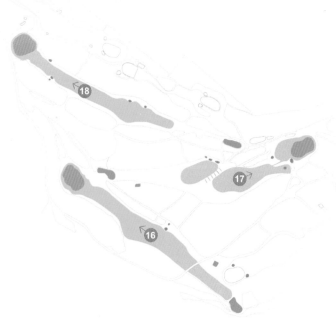

Play may finish but the experience will last forever.

The 16th climbs all the way back to the upper plateau, to a classic 'skyline' green. The public beach is to your left and you can see kites and hear the laughter of children as you play. You are almost home but then the 17th routes you backwards and down, into a secret hollow, from which you must hit up to yet another superb mid-level green. The 18th plays along the upper plateau and is more demanding than charming, playing as a par 5 for most people. It is a fine finishing hole but usually too hard for one to have to think of playing it in four strokes.

The 16th reminds you that most of Dornoch lies on "common good" land, owned by the people and leased to the club. On the tee you will often have to wait for oblivious ramblers to wend their way to safety on the path along the beach, and the benches between the green and the beach will be filled with holiday makers on a sunny day. Kites might even be flying over the green as you prepare for your approach.

272
272
263

103
corner

* 150

395   387
402

171

209
209
200

16 *High Hole*

■□ 402 ■ 395 ■ 387 • Par 4

The 16th is an uphill climb to a largely featureless skyline green. Many people feel it is the weakest hole on the course, but Peter Allis has called it the epitome of links golf, due to its intimation of infinity. The hole is a superb test of driving, both in strategy and execution. If you stray even a little to the left your ball can boomerang off a slope to the oblivion of an old quarry. If you bail out right there are two fairway bunkers which will guarantee a five.

A long iron or 3-wood to the left hand side, short of the quarry, is the safe shot. This leaves a blind uphill second for which distance control is difficult. The green is large, flat and fast, and protected by three large mounds on the right and a large hollow at the rear. Once on the green take a moment to enjoy one of the most beautiful panoramic views anywhere in golf.

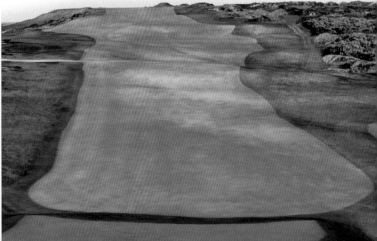

When Greg Norman first played the course he asked his caddie how to play the tee shot. "A draw over the marker post" was the laconic reply. "I see it as a fade over the bunkers," said Greg. After a bit more to-ing and fro-ing, Norman hit the caddy's shot, perfectly of course, but then asked to try his shot too. After another perfect execution, they walked to the brow of the hill and saw two balls no more than 5 feet apart, in position 'A' 80 yards short of the green...

162
220
220
206
200
145
94

405
390 384

200

165
marker
post

150

253
253
239
233

214

17 Valley

■□405 ■390 ■384 • Par 4

Similar in design to the 8th hole and equally charming. A blind tee shot can be played one of two ways. Firstly, you can drive a little left of the marker post to a lower fairway that will shorten your approach. Do not use your driver down wind as you may run out of fairway, or face a very long second if you push your drive right. Alternatively, you can lay up with an iron short of the bunkers on the upper fairway. This will leave a longer second but you will be looking down onto the green. If you opt for the first method then you will be left with a semi blind shot to the raised green. The most important thing is to carry the slope and the bunkers in front of the green and your ball should roll towards the bowl like putting surface. Favour the left as it gathers in more on this side.

Valley

If you opt for the lay up off the tee then you will
see the green in front and below you. If you play
towards the left half of the green you will see the
ball move down the slope and to the right, towards
the middle of the green.

Although this is a big, sloping green, it does not
break as much as you might think particularly
towards the back.

Being the 18th, there are many stories of achievement and despair, but these are more of the battle against attrition than of glory. A Par 4 is rarely scored on this hole when one needs one. The rare birdies come too often at the end of an indifferent round.

One of the most interesting shots ever seen on the 18th fairway was back across to the 2nd green, after someone playing the 2nd hole shanked off the tee in an important match.

150

200

302
302
294
291

207

233

220
220
211
207

456 446 442

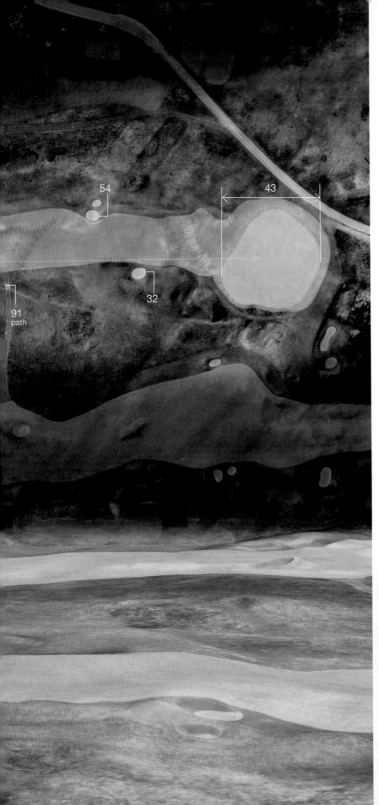

18 *Home*

■□456 ■446 ■442 • Par 4

A brute of a finishing hole whose charm is that it is a great test of golf, particularly at the end of a round. If you need a four at this hole and you get it, you have earned whatever you have won. It requires a long and straight tee shot, as close to the right hand bunkers as possible, but no matter where you finish, the second will be at least partially blind as the green is obscured by a small ridge 100 yards or so from the green.

The green itself is set in a wee hollow, but partially raised, leaving a wide 2-3 foot dip in the front. This means a shot that doesn't quite carry to the green can stop dead. Always take one more club on this hole, and if you see your approach shot bounce up you will know you have hit the green. The green itself has lots of slopes, humps and hollows, and many great pin positions, particularly short right.

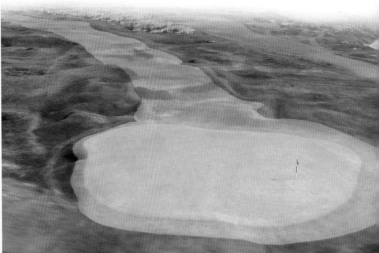

My Experiences

This last section is a conclusion to the book and a place where you may want to record your shots and scores to keep as a reminder of your time at Royal Dornoch. We hope that you have enjoyed the experience.

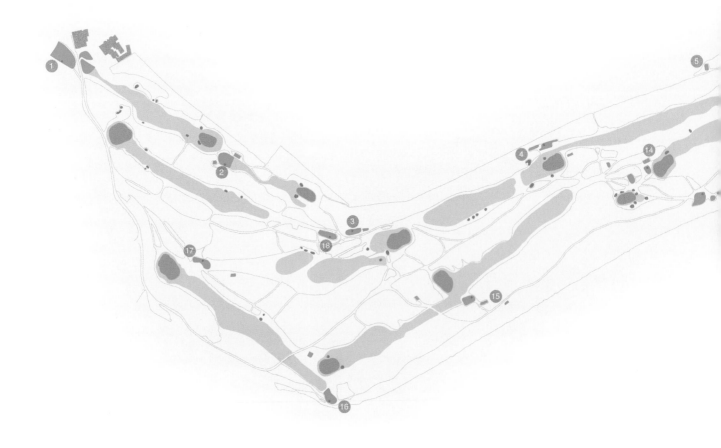

Draw in your shots to the greens above and mark your putts, flag positions and scores on the following pages.

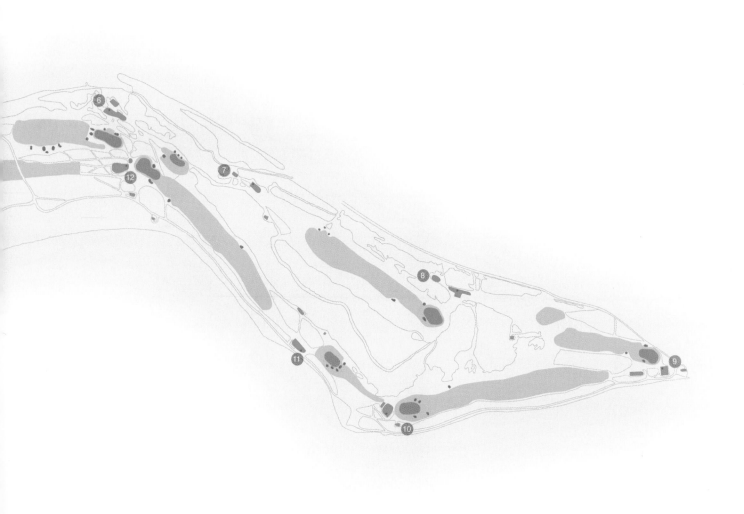

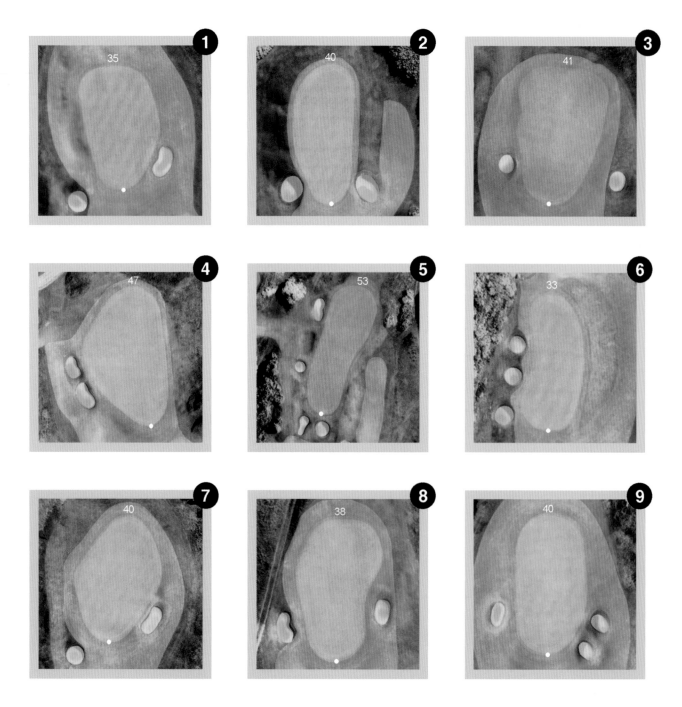

Mark your putts and flag positions on each green.

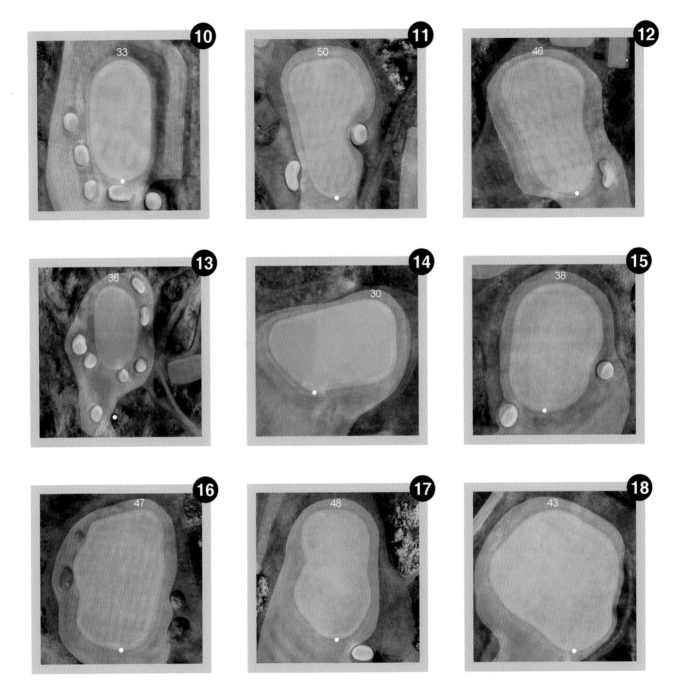

Competition:								🛡	Please indicate which tee used

Competition:

Date: Time:

Player: Handicap Strokes Rec'd

Hole	Blue Tees	Yellow Tees	White Tees	Red Tees	Par	Stroke Index			
1 First	331	331	300	266	4	7			
2 Ord	184	177	167	163	3	15			
3 Earl's Cross	414	414	398	389	4	11/1			
4 Achinchanter	427	427	403	391	4/5	3/9			
5 Hilton	354	354	317	311	4	9/3			
6 Whinny Brae	163	163	163	135	3	17			
7 Pier	463	463	423	412	4/5	1/11			
8 Dunrobin	437	396	386	380	4	5			
9 Craiglaith	529	496	491	435	5	13			
OUT	3302	3321	3048	2882	35/37	OUT			
10 Fuaran	177	147	142	137	3	16			
11 A'chlach	450	446	434	426	4/5	4/8			
12 Sutherland	507	507	489	472	5	12/4			
13 Bents	180	166	148	137	3	18			
14 Foxy	445	445	439	401	4/5	2			
15 Stulaig	358	319	298	288	4	10			
16 High Hole	402	402	395	387	4/5	6/12			
17 Valley	405	405	390	384	4	8/6			
18 Home	456	456	446	442	4/5	14			
IN	3380	3293	3181	3074	35/39	IN			
OUT	3302	3221	3048	2882	35/37	OUT			
TOTAL	6682	6514	6229	5956	70/76	TOTAL			